Shrimps for Beginners

ALINA DARIA

Copyright © 2022 Alina Daria

All rights reserved.

ISBN: 9798366353106

Contents

General Information 7

Five Popular Species...13

Gender and Reproduction...............................26

Purchasing Pet Shrimps 31

The Tank..37

Cycling Phase...45

Carbon Dioxide (CO2) 51

Socialisation 54

Diet and Nutrition..60

Behaviour...71

Diseases and Health Risks 76

Frequently Asked Questions 81

Legal Notice...97

Room for Notes..99

General Information

Shrimp are becoming increasingly popular as pets and are moving into more and more living rooms around the world! Whereas in the past aquarists were mainly enthusiastic about fish or even amphibians as pets, the interest in invertebrates such as shrimps is always growing, and shrimps inspire many animal lovers. In this book, we will focus on shrimp living in freshwater aquariums.

First, let's take a closer look at the taxonomic classification of shrimp. Shrimps belong to the phylum Arthropoda and therein to the subphylum Crustacea.

Subsequently, they are assigned to the class of higher crustaceans (Malacostraca) and to the order of decapods (Decapoda). Crabs and hermit crabs, for example, also belong to this order, but shrimps represent a separate, quite distinct suborder: the Caridea! This group of animals was established in 1852 by the US zoologist James Dwight Dana.

Fascinatingly, there are about 3,000 different crustaceans - and more than 2,500 of them are shrimps! We can already see how diverse shrimp are. However, there are also species that are commonly called "shrimp", but strictly speaking do not belong to the suborder Caridea shrimp (such as the species Aristeus antennatus, which has a tree-shaped branched gill structure, in contrast to the shrimp of the suborder Caridea, which have a flat gill structure).

It should also be noted that the majority of shrimp species live in oceans. We do not deal with these species, as this is a book about freshwater shrimp. We will deal with them in more detail and take a closer look at the aquarium keeping of these species.

In general, it can be stated that shrimp in the wild live mainly near the coast in summer, while in winter they tend to move to deeper waters. The size of different shrimp species varies, sometimes greatly, and also depends on how warm or cold the particular body of water is in which they live. The warmer the water, the larger the shrimp.

Shrimp feed on a variety of animal and plant remains - this is the main reason why they have long been popular in aquariums, as they are commonly considered to be useful algae eliminators.

© *Basuka*

Shrimp belong to the aquatic animals that hardly swim. They do not use fins for locomotion like fish, but their legs. Shrimp have ten legs, which can be seen from the fact that they belong to the order of decapod crustaceans, as explained earlier.

For locomotion, they mainly use their hind legs, by means of which they can walk over the ground or climb over something; in addition, many species have claws on their front legs, with which they can grasp small objects, for example.

Whether shrimp mate with each other depends on the species. For example, theoretically all shrimp of the Neocaridina group can interbreed. Likewise, all shrimp of the Caridina group can mate. However, a Neocaridina shrimp cannot mate with a Caridina shrimp.

© Denise Gugler - DehliLabutta

Five Popular Species

As we have already noted, there are an overwhelming number of different shrimp species. So, which ones are suitable for a freshwater aquarium at home?

To answer this question, we will now take a closer look at five particularly popular species. It also plays a role whether it should be a pure shrimp aquarium without fish or whether a fish aquarium is supplemented by shrimp.

If shrimps are to live together with fish, it is particularly important to ensure that all creatures living in the aquarium have approximately the same requirements for water temperature, vegetation in the aquarium and other parameters, so that all living creatures - whether fish or shrimps - can be provided with a species-appropriate and natural way of life.

© *Envandrare*

Cherry Shrimp, Red Cherry Shrimp

Scientific name: Neocaridina davidi

Red cherry shrimp are among the most popular shrimp in aquariums around the globe. This species gets its name from its wonderful red coloration, of course, but there are also blue morphs, for example. Red fire shrimp belong to the dwarf shrimp, and it has been used as an algae eater for a long time.

These animals are very suitable for beginners because they are not very sensitive and fit into many different freshwater aquariums. Especially with medium sized tropical freshwater fishes red fire shrimp get along very well. They are native to the areas of China, Taiwan and the like. Breeding is also relatively uncomplicated, and the animals usually live between one and a half and two years.

Size: 2.5 to 3 centimeters (1 to 1.2 inches)

Water temperature: 22°C to 28°C (72°F to 82°F)

Required pH-value: 6 to 8

Required total water hardness: 4 to 14 GH

Nitrate value: less than 20 ppm

Carbonate hardness: 1 to 8 KH

TDS value ("Total Dissolved Solids"): 80 to 400

Space requirement: at least 40 liters (9 gallons)

Yamato shrimp, Japanese shrimp, Amano shrimp, Algae shrimp

Scientific name: Caridina multidentata

Yamato shrimps are also a very popular shrimp in the home aquarium, which also remain quite small, but is usually somewhat larger than the previously presented species. Yamato shrimp has its home in the Japanese waters, and it is very suitable for beginners, as it is not particularly demanding in terms of nutrition; it also keeps the aquarium free of algae.

Another reason why this species is well suited for beginners who are not interested in breeding is the fact that reproduction is rather difficult. Yamato shrimps are said to have a friendly nature and an uncomplicated character, but they should be kept in a group of at least six shrimp to avoid too dominant behavior.

Size: 3 to 6 centimeters (1.2 to 2.4 inches)

Water temperature: 18°C to 28°C (64°F to 82°F)

Required pH value: 6.5 to 8

Required total water hardness: 5 to 15 GH

Nitrate value: less than 20 ppm

Carbonate hardness: 1 to 8 KH

TDS (Total Dissolved Solids) value: 100 to 400

Available space: at least 40 liters (9 gallons)

Bamboo Shrimp

Scientific name: Atyopsis moluccensis

This shrimp species has its home in the waters of Southeast Asia and is therefore (also) dependent on fairly warm water. Every few months a Bamboo shrimp gets rid of its exoskeleton. The exoskeleton serves for stabilization and is, so to speak, an outer skeleton (we humans have an inner skeleton, i.e., an endoskeleton).

They are also quite friendly and not particularly aggressive animals, so they are well suited for beginners and for many different aquariums.

Size: about ten centimeters (4 inches)

Water temperature: 22°C to 28°C (72°F to 82°F)

Required pH value: 6 to 8

Required total water hardness: 6 to 8 GH

Nitrate value: less than 20 ppm

Carbonate hardness: 2 to 6 KH

TDS (Total Dissolved Solids) value: 100 to 400

Space requirement: at least 80 liters (18 gallons)

Striped Bumblebee Shrimp

Scientific name: Gnathophyllum americanum

From the name it can already be deduced that these animals are striped shrimp, whose stripes resemble a bumblebee (colors: yellow and black).

This shrimp species originates from bays, tropical lagoons and reefs. IMPORTANT: The genus Gnathophyllidae was established in 1852 by James Dwight Dana but was declared invalid in 2015.

This was done by scientists De Grave, Fransen and Page, who believe that this genus should be considered a synonym of the family Palaemonidae.

They belong to the dwarf shrimps and love dense vegetation and small caves. Their keeping turns out to be a little more difficult or more elaborate than the keeping of the previously presented species, since the values in the aquarium have to be kept quite accurately and must not fluctuate very much - this can be seen from the values below, whose tolerance limits are narrower than those of the other species.

Size: maximum 4 centimeters (1.6 inches)

Water temperature: 20°C to 26°C (68°F to 78°F)

Required pH: 6.2 to 6.8 pH

Required total water hardness: 4 to 6 GH

Nitrate value: less than 20 ppm

Carbonate hardness: 0 to 2 KH

TDS (Total Dissolved Solids) value: 100 to 180

Available space: at least 40 liters (9 gallons)

Bee Shrimp

Scientific name: Caridina cantonensis

This shrimp species usually lives about one to two years. It is native to the waters of southern China and Taiwan. They are dependent on soft water. Due to the diverse color patterns, these shrimp are always and increasingly popular in domestic aquariums.

However, it must be said that bee shrimp are not the easiest shrimp to keep and for beginners, the previously introduced species are more suitable while you are still in the learning process. Often aquarists acquire bee shrimp when they have already gained some experience.

Size: 2.5 to 3 centimeters (1 to 1.2 inches)

Water temperature: 21°C to 23°C (70°F to 73°F)

Required pH: 6.2 to 7.2 pH

Required total water hardness: 3 to 7 GH

Nitrate value: less than 20 ppm

Carbonate hardness: 0 to 4 KH

TDS (Total Dissolved Solids) value: 100 to 250

Available space: at least 40 liters (9 gallons)

© *Neocaridina Blue Dream – Saviera*

Gender and Reproduction

Whether shrimp will mate with each other depends on the species. For example, theoretically all shrimp of the Neocaridina group can interbreed. Likewise, all shrimp of the Caridina group can mate. However, a Neocaridina shrimp cannot mate with a Caridina shrimp.

At which point of time a shrimp reaches sexual maturity depends on the species. Generally, most female shrimp become sexually mature at about three months of age. Depending on how old they are, they will lay about 15 to 40 eggs. If fertilization of the eggs has occurred, the offspring hatch from their eggs after about 14 to 21 days.

Most shrimp are so teeny tiny after hatching that they can hardly be seen with the naked eye. The colorful appearance they get only later. Many aquarists even use a magnifying glass to spot the babies. One species that reproduces particularly easily and quickly is the Neocaridina. Therefore, Neocaridina shrimp are often recommended for beginners in keeping and/or breeding. In addition, they are not particularly demanding of their environment and are rather hardy.

When it is time for mating, the females emit a pheromone to signal the males that they are ready to mate. The males then become somewhat restless and go in search of a female with which to mate.

Once mating is complete and the eggs have been fertilized, they are quite easy to spot on the females. Usually, the eggs are greenish or white yellowish. Over time, the eggs become darker and darker.

Whether the baby shrimp, which are initially barely visible to the naked eye, will survive depends on many factors, including whether there are fish in the aquarium. Baby shrimps are often eaten by fish. Moss, for example, is a good hiding place for the small shrimp.

As a rule, females have a fuller and rounder body structure than males. In them the "plates" of their abdominal segments continue further down, and the head carapace also protrudes somewhat further down, but for the layperson this is usually not easy to recognize. As the animals get older, the differences become more obvious.

In addition, in some shrimp you can see the ovaries of the females, which are located approximately at the level of the neck; more precisely, on the dorsal side behind the stomach of the shrimp. This is accomplished quite well in species that are somewhat translucent. What color the eggs themselves are also varies from species to species; for example, the eggs can be red, yellow, brown, white, or green depending on the species.

Females are usually not only rounder and more fully built than males, but differences in size can also be seen, again depending on the species. In Macrobrachium shrimp, the males are often larger than the females. Furthermore, it can be observed that in Macrobrachium shrimp the females often have smaller claw legs and smaller pincers than the males.

In Caridina shrimp it is the opposite and the females are often larger. However, this is only the rule, and it does not always have to be that way.

© Ishman000

Purchasing Pet Shrimps

At the outset, I would like to point out that shrimp should not be purchased until their new home is completed and ready for them. Many new aquarists do not consider (or know) that an aquarium must first complete the cycling phase before fish, amphibians or shrimp can move in.

We will come back to this topic later, because in the cycling phase of a new aquarium, nitrate and nitrate levels will first rise sharply and then fall again - if the animals are put into an aquarium too early, there is a risk of poisoning. This phase varies in length, but often lasts between four and six weeks. During this time, the water values must already be tested regularly.

Even if an aquarium already exists - for example, a fish aquarium whose parameters are suitable for the desired shrimp species - the animals should not be added immediately but should serve a quarantine period of about four weeks to ensure that the shrimp do not introduce any pathogens into the aquarium.

How expensive shrimp are depends greatly on their abundance and characteristics. Particularly beautiful ornamental shrimp are the most expensive, for example, Crystal Red shrimp.

If one wants to acquire pets, the first way leads most people to a pet shop. However, it should be noted that pet shops are commercial enterprises that want to make a profit and sell their products. This also includes the animals. For this reason, there are quite a few pet shops that neither keep their animals in a species-appropriate manner nor obtain them from reputable breeders. Of course, this does not apply to all stores equally; there are definitely pet shops that attach a lot of importance to the health and well-being of the animals and that also train their employees accordingly. Many salespeople are not adequately trained and often do not know the individual animal species well enough to be able to provide competent advice. Of course, there are exceptions, and many sellers make a great effort - but you should be careful.

Unhealthy shrimps are often not easy to recognize for a layperson, but usually sluggishness and a pale coloration indicate possible diseases.

It is a good idea to source pets regionally and keep transport distances as short and convenient as possible.

There are enough reputable breeders who are happy to explain the needs of the animals to newcomers and to provide advice. After all, a good breeder also wants his animals to get into good hands and not to waste away. Furthermore, reputable breeders are usually better contacts than the staff in pet shops, because they are real experts in their field and know their respective species inside out.

At many breeders you can visit shrimps first. Thereby you should pay attention to whether the animals are kept species-appropriate and whether they look healthy. The shrimps should have enough space, they should move lively, not show any injuries, not look pale and generally look fit.

Of course, another option is to adopt shrimp. There are enough pets - not only shrimp - but that are also no longer wanted by their previous owners or have to leave their previous home for other reasons. Unfortunately, these animals are often abandoned in public waters such as ponds, where they usually die. These animals also have the right to a nice life. Therefore, adoption is often a good idea.

If the shrimp of a new group are obtained from different sources or if stragglers are to enrich an existing group, a quarantine should be carried out first (about four weeks).

In quarantine the shrimp can first recover, and the shrimp can be better observed to exclude that it has diseases that could be transmitted to the other animals without quarantine.

© *Neocaridina Blue Dream - Andreas Poznanski - Unlike-You-Photography*

The Tank

The minimum size of an aquarium for shrimp varies somewhat - for example, it also depends on whether the shrimp are to live in an aquarium with other co-inhabitants (fish) or whether it is a pure species aquarium in which only shrimp are kept.

If shrimp live together with fish, it depends of course on the total number of animals and the space requirements of the fish. Therefore, we focus here on species-pure aquariums in which only shrimp live. Even for small shrimp in smaller groups, at least 40 liters (9 gallons) of space should be provided so that the shrimp have enough free space. Some species such as Atyopsis moluccensis, which is one of the larger species, should have at least 80 liters (18 gallons) of space available.

I am aware that an aquarium with a capacity of 20 liters (4.5 gallons) is often recommended for dwarf shrimp. In my experience, however, this is too small, as even small animals like shrimp should have enough space to explore and move around. I therefore recommend 40 liters as a minimum size.

For example, different species of dwarf shrimp can also be socialized with each other, but one should truly not overdo it. The less species are mixed, the better are the chances for an uncomplicated and permanently low complication keeping. The name "dwarf shrimp" already suggests that these shrimp belong to the smaller variety: So, if they are not to be kept in a species aquarium, but socialized with fish, they must be small and peaceful fish only.

If you decide to keep dwarf shrimp, a group of about 10-15 is a good idea. They are very sociable.

If they are to live together with small fish, guppies or platies are suitable, for example.

Macrobrachium shrimp, on the other hand, should not be socialized with fish, but should live in a species-specific aquarium. With Atyopsis it depends - they can possibly be kept together with larger fish, but safer and more peaceful coexistence is rather in a species aquarium. At least this way of keeping is best for newbies at the beginning.

Atyopsis are also suitable if you do not want the shrimp to reproduce. The larvae of Atyopsis grow up in brackish water (i.e., in a mixture of fresh and salt water) in nature, therefore reproduction does not usually occur in the home aquarium. With Atyopsis, the group does not have to be as large as with dwarf shrimp - a group of five, for example, is sufficient for the start.

Among the most dominant shrimp are the Macrobrachium shrimp, which should rather be kept in pairs or in a very small group. Especially the males are very dominant and only want to live together with a few females - if it comes to competition, this can lead to fierce fights.

The shrimp aquarium should not be open, but closed, otherwise there is a risk that the shrimp will jump or climb out of the aquarium.

© Kaarok

Special care should be taken with the water filter, because although it is important for the water quality, a filter can, if necessary, suck the water so strongly that a shrimp could disappear in it and fall victim to the filter. Therefore, the filter opening should be covered.

The temperature of the water should be based on the temperature that prevails in the waters of origin of the shrimp species in question. For many shrimp species, a temperature of about 24-25°C (75-77°F) is a good guideline. The exact temperature limits for some popular species are listed in the "Popular Species" section. The same applies to pH levels and other parameters.

The aquarium is always cleaned by the shrimp themselves and by the filter, but to remove pollutants, a small water change should be done regularly. Many aquarists change about 20% of the water every one to two weeks. The filter should preferably be a sponge filter.

In addition to naturally developing algae, Java moss, Dwarf Ambulia, Vallisneria and Anubias are also very suitable plants in the shrimp aquarium.

Shrimp like to hide, so it is recommended to offer them plenty of hiding places. These hiding places can be plants as well as stones, small caves or other decorative material. On stones and decorative objects can also live microorganisms and algae, on which shrimps feed among other things.

For substrate, most aquarists choose gravel or sand for their shrimp aquarium. A substrate is important and should not be done without (i.e., no bare bottom), as valuable bacteria collect in the bottom substrate.

The pH level in the shrimp aquarium should be between about 6.5 and 8, although this can vary depending on the species. Some exact values can be found in the "Popular Species" chapter.

When shrimp are happy and thriving, they often give birth to offspring. It is very interesting to watch them carry the eggs around and take care of them until they hatch. However, the little baby shrimp are hard to see with the naked eye; many aquarists use a magnifying glass.

© *Basuka*

Cycling Phase

The so-called cycling phase is essential for every aquarium! In this phase, a natural balance is first established in the aquarium before the shrimp can move into their new home. In the cycling phase, the tank develops a natural habitat and healthy water levels are achieved. The water will outgas during this phase and clear of turbidity and suspended solids over time. The essential good bacteria will slowly form and accumulate mainly at the bottom and in the filter.

There are still people who start up an aquarium, including shrimp, without first having it complete its cycle. This is usually done out of ignorance and often due to lack of education in the pet shop. A serious breeder will educate every newcomer about the cycling phase, as it is especially important for the health of the shrimp.

How long the cycling phase lasts is very individual and depends on various factors - for example, the total water volume and the plants used. However, it is important to be patient, as this phase requires at least four weeks. Most aquariums are ready for the new inhabitants between about four and eight weeks.

The aquarium is first prepared and put into operation without inserting the shrimp. The substrate is rinsed off - under the shower, for example - and the bottom is covered to about two to six centimeters throughout (1-3 inches). The plants are already inserted, as they play a major role in the development of the balance in the tank. Any decorative items, such as large stones or roots, can also already be added to the aquarium. The water is let in, and the filter is put into operation. It is important that the filter is already running during the cycling phase.

Usually, water changes are not necessary during this phase. However, many keepers perform a fifty percent water change after about three weeks. This allows pollutants in the water to be eliminated more quickly.

It is possible that the aquatic plants may become somewhat stunted or even die during the cycling phase, as the water values are not yet good. However, the plants should not be removed from the tank as they play a major role in establishing the natural balance. If necessary, the plants can be replaced after the cycling phase is over.

During the cycling phase, the water values are checked regularly. The most critical value is the nitrite value. This will slowly increase and reach a peak at a certain point in time - the so-called "nitrite peak". It is very difficult to predict when this will occur. Sometimes the nitrite peak occurs after just one week, but sometimes it takes six weeks. The most important thing is to actually wait for the peak, be patient and don't let the shrimp move in too soon; because nitrite is extremely harmful to shrimp and other aquatic life. It enters the bloodstream, where it prevents (or impedes) the smooth transport of oxygen. Nitrite can poison shrimp and cause other diseases. This is another reason why it is so important to always keep an eye on the water values. Nitrite should not be detectable in the water or, in the worst case, should rise to a maximum of 0.5 mg per liter (0.5 ppm) - then a large water change should be performed immediately.

When the nitrite peak is reached, the level will slowly decrease again. The peak usually lasts a few days, sometimes a week. When the nitrite level drops steadily and eventually become undetectable, the tank is usually ready for the animals to move in.

Nitrite poisoning in shrimp can be recognized, for example, by the shrimp only sluggishly lolling around on the substrate and hardly eating. Nitrite poisoning is particularly easy to recognize in transparent shrimp species, as the muscles of the abdomen change color (often milky-white or milky-orange).

© *loilamtan - bruce lam*

Carbon Dioxide (CO2)

Since most freshwater shrimp live in fairly warm water, care must be taken to ensure that there is always sufficient oxygen in the tank. The warmer the water, the less oxygen it contains. Oxygen is removed from the water by the shrimp's respiration and the shrimp exhale CO2. The CO2 content depends accordingly on the size of the aquarium, the stocking and the number of plants.

If too many shrimp (and possibly fish) have to share a too small aquarium, the CO2 content in the water is naturally higher, since more animals release CO2 into the water.

The aquatic plants then convert the CO2 back into oxygen. This is another reason why it is important that the tank is sufficiently planted! CO_2 also promotes plant growth, but too much CO_2 is toxic for the animals, as they no longer have enough oxygen. In the worst case they can suffocate.

Therefore, especially beginners should keep their hands off CO_2 systems! These are needed for particularly sensitive plants to promote and maintain their growth. For a simple shrimp aquarium, however, simple plants such as Java moss, Vallisneria and similar plants are suitable. If one resorts to such undemanding plants and does without a CO_2 system, the risk of CO_2 poisoning can be very easily eliminated.

Regular water changes also bring fresh oxygen into the aquarium. Regarding the water filter, it is recommended to place the pipe just below the water surface, so that it is always slightly in motion and enriches the water with new oxygen. However, good care must be taken to cover the filter opening so that the shrimp are not sucked in.

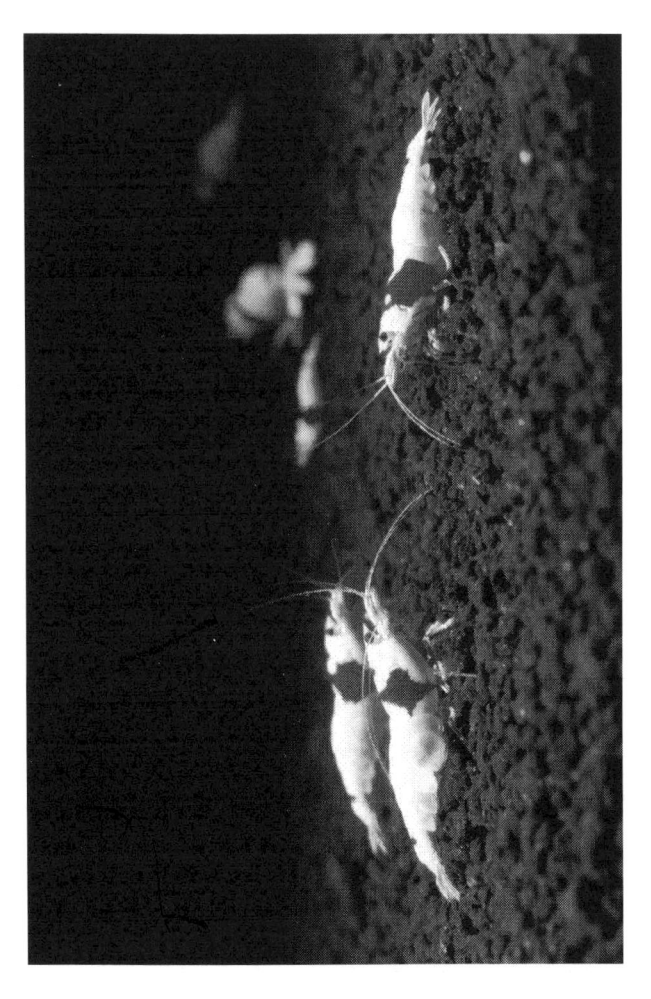

© Ishman000

Socialisation

We have already briefly discussed in a previous chapter that shrimp can live together with fish in an aquarium under certain circumstances. If a mixed aquarium is desired rather than a pure species aquarium, some points must be considered. These include, for example, that the requirements for parameters such as temperature must be similar for all species and that neither the fish hurt the shrimp nor vice versa. So, it all comes down to the correct mix.

There is never a guarantee that the composition will work or fail. Therefore, the following rules are not set in stone - there can always be exceptions, but we are looking at common experience here. It is not possible to give a hundred percent guarantee of successful coexistence, as no universal compatibility exists.

Fish that should rather not be put together with shrimps, as the risk is very high that the fish would eat the shrimps, are for example the following:

- Cichlids

- Rainbow fish

- Labyrinth fish or climbing fish

- Carp-like fish

- Boraras

- Rasboras

- Danios

- Puffer fish

Fish that usually live well and peacefully together with shrimps are for example:

- Endler guppies
- Trigonostigma
- Algae eaters
- Small tetra species
- Otocinclus
- Ancistrus
- Small Corydoras
- Loricaria

Even though fish that feed on animal protein such as shrimp in the wild are accustomed to pellets and similar foods in the aquarium, the hunting instinct in them will revive when they are presented with shrimp.

A common rule of thumb is that fish with a large mouth that shrimp can fit into should not live with them. However, there are also aggressive smaller fish that have a small mouth into which a shrimp cannot easily fit, but which can physically harass a shrimp to the point that the shrimp's legs break off, leaving it defenseless to be eaten by the fish. This is the case with small puffer fish, for example.

Inconspicuous shrimps, which do not have splendid colors, escape the fish longer, especially if they are offered enough hiding places. But let's face it - we don't want our shrimp to be eaten, do we? Therefore, we should make sure from the beginning that we only put fish and shrimp together that match each other and get along well.

It also happens that some fish species eat the shrimp eggs. This can be observed, for example, with neon tetras.

Nevertheless, hiding places should always be provided, especially for baby shrimp. Moss is a very popular hiding place for shrimp, which furthermore contributes to a natural biotope.

Furthermore, care should be taken that there is always enough food in the aquarium and that the aquarium is not overcrowded; all inhabitants should therefore have enough space and freedom, otherwise this can lead to aggression and general dissatisfaction, which can cause fights.

Furthermore, it should also be considered that not only fish can attack shrimp - but the reverse can also occur. This is especially often observed with Macrobrachium shrimp, which can grow up to thirty centimeters and often attack or eat small fish.

© *Lysmata Debelius - LaDameBucolique*

Diet and Nutrition

We have already discussed that shrimp were initially particularly popular with aquarists because they eat algae, among other things, and thereby keep an aquarium nice and clean. Since there are so many different shrimp species, their diet also differs depending on their place of origin, but in general it can be stated that the diet is based on algae, other plants and bacteria. However, in addition, there are also, for example, foliage, cuttlebone and the like - let's take a closer look at this.

In nature, shrimp are scavengers, which search the waters in which they live for algae, bacteria, plants and the like. Sometimes they also eat dead fish or another dead shrimp, if they find them during their search.

Accordingly, the diet consists mainly of plant food and is supplemented with animal protein on occasion. However, animal protein is far from being the staple diet of shrimp, so some feeds offered in pet food stores are not particularly species-appropriate, as they often contain far too high a percentage of animal protein.

Algae:

Algae are the staple food for shrimp in nature. Therefore, they should also be offered algae (among other things) to eat in the home aquarium, on which they can constantly pick around. This not only benefits the shrimp themselves, but also keeps the aquarium clean. If the shrimp become restless and nervously wander through the aquarium, they will probably not find any algae or other food. If algae develop in the aquarium, but the shrimp do not eat them, this may be because they are fed "too much" other food and therefore do not use the algae as food. In this case, it may be useful to take a short feeding break of one to two days until the shrimp have eaten their fill of algae.

Vegetables:

No question - vegetables are naturally not found in the waters where shrimp normally live, so vegetables are not essential for a species-appropriate shrimp diet. Nevertheless, there are many aquarists who occasionally offer their shrimp bits of vegetables for variety. These include cucumbers, spinach, zucchini, carrots, broccoli or kale. If vegetables are fed, be sure to remove the peel beforehand; and cut the vegetables into small pieces, approximately one inch in size. Many aquarists cook hard vegetables in advance (without salt or spices, of course) to make it a little easier for the shrimp to eat, as the cooking process softens the vegetables. However, if the shrimp do not eat the vegetables, for example because they do not like them or because too much food was offered, the leftovers should be removed from the aquarium the next day. Nevertheless, it should be pointed out that feeding vegetables is not approved by all aquarists, since they are not part of the natural diet and since carrots, for example, can pollute the water. In addition, many vegetables are contaminated with pesticides, which can be a danger especially for the small shrimp body and for the biotope in the aquarium. Accordingly, if vegetables are fed, organic quality should be considered.

Foliage:

Foliage? In the aquarium? As food for shrimps? Actually yes! And feeding foliage is not unnatural either, since in the wild foliage also falls into the waters where shrimp live. Therefore, foliage does contribute to a natural habitat and to a species-appropriate diet. When tree leaves decay, infusoria grow on them - this is a collection of harmless bacteria as well as other microorganisms that serve as food for shrimp. Many aquarists collect foliage from their surroundings, such as nearby forests. The foliage should be dry and clean - and of course it should not have come into contact with pesticides or fertilizers. Foliage from your own garden or from public forests is therefore a good choice. In addition, Indian sea almond leaves are also very popular in various types of aquariums, as these leaves secrete flavonoids and tannins, which have been shown to have anti-inflammatory and antimicrobial effects. This is another advantage of Indian sea almond tree leaves.

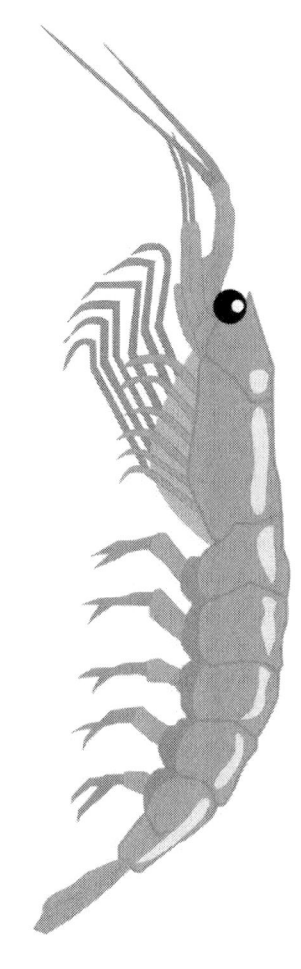

© *Mostafa Elturkey*

Some examples of brown fall foliage that can be used for the aquarium:

- Apple tree

- Birch

- Oak tree

- Hornbeam

- Hazel

- Norway maple

- Elm

- Willow

Cuttlebone:

For calcium supply, many aquarists resort to cuttlebone. Cuttlebone comes from squid and is available in various forms, as it is also fed to reptiles, for example, which also rely heavily on an adequate supply of calcium. While reptiles are usually offered a cuttlebone powder, for shrimp one usually uses a block from which smaller pieces are broken off. In pet stores, cuttlebone is usually found in the bird section, as it is also commonly used for birds to ensure an adequate supply of calcium - especially for healthy growth and complication-free egg laying.

Industrially produced shrimp food:

Most aquarists avoid industrially produced shrimp feed, as this often involves mixing unhealthy additives (for example, as fillers or waste in order to still market them for profit) into the feed. In addition, many feeds contain too much animal protein, as shrimp in nature feed almost exclusively on vegetable food and only consume animal protein if they happen to find it (e.g., dead fish or other dead shrimp). The reason why companies usually use too much animal protein in their feed is that crab meat and fish meal are cheaper than spirulina or other algae. This is about profit and not about the species-appropriate nutrition of the animals. Therefore, you should definitely pay attention to the composition if you want to use industrially produced feed. The basis of this feed should be algae.

Herbs:

Herbs can also be gladly fed to the shrimp. Herbs can be home-grown, purchased or collected from forests. They should be washed before feeding to avoid introducing contaminants or pathogens into the aquarium. The following herbs are good for feeding:

- Basil
- Nettle
- Daisies
- Dandelion

- Ribwort and common plantain

- Yarrow

- Chickweed

To prevent contamination of the water, food remains should be removed from the aquarium once a day.

© *Basuka*

Behaviour

Shrimp spend most of their time at the bottom. On the bottom they find food more easily and can hide better from dangers, such as predatory fish. They often use plants as hiding places.

We have already talked about the fact that shrimp even feed on bacteria, among other things, and therefore act as little cleaners - besides the fact that they also eat unwanted algae. In the wild, there are shrimp species that keep other marine animals such as fish clean in this way and in return are left alone or even protected by them.

Likewise, we have already learned that shrimp do not have an inner skeleton (endoskeleton) like humans, for example, but only an exoskeleton (outer skeleton). This is also called the carapace. The carapace not only protects the shrimp, but it also gives them the ability to move around the aquarium. However, since the carapace does not grow with the shrimp as it gets larger, the animal must shed its skin regularly. This does not always go smoothly and sometimes there are problems with molting, which in the worst case can lead to the death of the animal. Also, for this reason, care should always be taken that the environment is as species-appropriate and natural as possible (water values as in the home waters) and that the shrimp are supplied with all nutrients.

As a rule, shrimp move around on foot, i.e., walking on the substrate. Sometimes they swim but walking is their preferred form of locomotion. They are rather leisurely animals, moving quite slowly and smoothly - if there is any bustle, it is possible that something is wrong with their living conditions.

However, if shrimp just sit around without moving, this is also a sign that something might be wrong - for example, that the water values are poor. However, they naturally become calmer when, for example, they are pressing eggs or when the next molt is imminent.

Shrimp are social animals and live in groups in nature. They are not solitary animals. Therefore, they should not have to live alone in the home aquarium and always need conspecifics. It is possible to keep different species of shrimp together, as long as the species get along well and live together peacefully, but you should house about ten to fifteen shrimp of each species. This is a good guideline. More shrimp are possible, of course - it depends on the size of the aquarium. If different shrimp species live together, they must of course be species that also live in similar circumstances in nature and have similar requirements for water values.

Female shrimp will develop eggs that can later be fertilized by males during the "mating swim." At this time, there is a lot of activity in the aquarium and the animals go in search of a suitable mate. The males are attracted by the pheromones secreted by the females and a chase often ensues, eventually ending in mating.

The eggs of the female are initially still in the neck of the animal and only after mating move to the abdominal area, where the female carries them around. There the fertilization takes place.

© *Red Fire - Claudia Wollesen*

Diseases and Health Risks

Relatively little is currently known about diseases in shrimp - at least compared to other pets such as fish. Every human being and every animal can fall ill; how often and how severe is always individual. In most cases, disease prevention is the most important criterion, because if the shrimp live under species-appropriate conditions and are fed a healthy diet, this can already contribute a lot to the health of the small animals.

As a rule, the majority of diseases and problems are due to polluted water quality or unnatural water values. Too few water changes are also common - or incorrect feeding.

The stronger a person's immune system, the less likely they are to get sick. It is similar with shrimp and other animals. Animals are protected by their immune systems, but stress and other strains can weaken the immune system, causing bad bacteria, parasites and fungi to become health hazards, possibly causing infections that in many cases spread quickly through the aquarium and can also infect any other tankmates such as fish.

If health problems occur, not only should the symptoms be combated, but the cause should be investigated. Causes of problems can be for example the following:

1. no or too few water changes
2. introduction of new animals without quarantine
3. cycling phase was not completed

4. food remains have not been removed and are rotting

5. no filter available or filter too dirty

Antibacterial leaves that can help well against infections (the leaves are eaten by the shrimp depending on the species, but the bacteria that develop on them over time are usually grazed off):

- Sea almond leaves (also called catappa tree; Terminalia catappa).

- Beech leaves

- Nettle leaves

In addition, willow bark can be used as a decorative material, as it also has an antibacterial effect. It lowers the germ density in the home aquarium and can be very helpful, since especially dwarf shrimp react very sensitively to too much germ pressure.

There is no general rule here, but experience shows that Caridina shrimp are more sensitive than Neocaridina shrimp.

Special attention should be paid to avoid poisoning in the aquarium. These can occur, for example, if the nitrite or nitrate values in the water are too high. Therefore, the water values should be tested regularly. Depending on the region, it is also possible that copper residues from the water pipe can get into the aquarium and thus cause poisoning.

Another possibility for poisoned water is that new plants are not rinsed off before being placed in the aquarium, thus introducing contaminants into the aquarium. If something rots in the substrate or if deceased shrimp are not removed from the aquarium, this can also extremely contaminate the water. If industrial feed is (also) used for feeding, it must of course be checked that the expiration date has not yet expired.

© *Basuka*

Frequently Asked Questions

My shrimp behave somehow differently after the water change. What can be the reason for this?

It is common for shrimp to want to reproduce after a water change, so they restlessly search for a mate. This is because shrimp see fluctuations in water temperature as a sign of reproduction. It is best if the fresh water is already about the same temperature as the aquarium water when it is filled.

If I offer foliage to my shrimp, do I need to let it dry first?

Yes, please. The collected foliage leaves should first be dried completely at home before they are added to the aquarium. Usually, the leaves will sink to the bottom after a few days.

Is it not possible that I introduce pathogens or small insects into my aquarium through the foliage?

Yes, this is possible. Therefore, it is a good idea to boil the leaves before using them. The heat kills (most) pathogens and small insects.

Which plants are particularly suitable for the shrimp aquarium?

The following plants are classics and very well suited for the shrimp aquarium:

- Algae ball / Moss ball (Aegagropila linnaei)

- Java moss (Taxiphyllum barbiere; formerly: Vesicularia dubyana)

- Anubias

- Small Ambulia (Limnophila sessiliflora)

- Microsorum pteropus

- Cryptocoryne wendtii

- Vallisneria americana

© *Basuka*

Which shrimp species are particularly suitable for a freshwater aquarium?

We have already taken a closer look at five popular species in the chapter "Popular species". In general, shrimp can be classified into several head categories, of which the following are particularly well suited for freshwater aquariums:

- Dwarf shrimp: These shrimp are exceedingly sociable and live harmoniously together, usually even when different species of dwarf shrimp are kept together. They usually reproduce quite rapidly with few complications.

- Atyopsis shrimp: These shrimp often like to stay near the water filter to absorb even more nutrients through this. They can usually be socialized well with dwarf shrimp and are also relatively peaceful. Unlike dwarf shrimp, however, these shrimp will not reproduce in the aquarium, as the larvae grow up in brackish water in the wild (i.e., in a mixture of freshwater and saltwater, which is of course not present in the aquarium).

- Macrobrachium shrimp: These shrimp are much more dominant and sometimes more aggressive than the shrimp mentioned above. In nature these shrimps are no loners, but their group usually consists of less shrimps, because the males only want to form a group with a few females and in case of competition they like to become aggressive and ready to fight.

Do I absolutely need a filter for my aquarium?

Yes, you should not do without a filter to ensure a good water quality at all times. However, care must be taken that the shrimp are not sucked in by the filter; this can be fatal. Sponge filters are best suited for shrimp aquariums, as they contain no moving parts and have a fine structure so that the shrimp cannot fit through them.

Does the filter also need to be cleaned?

Yes, approximately every few weeks. It is important not to use any cleaning agents. Some aquarists do not even use tap water for cleaning, but some aquarium water. The water is filled into a small bucket or similar and the sponge is carefully wrung out in this and thus freed from dirt. In this way, however, you ensure that the good bacteria that have accumulated in the filter are not lost.

How many shrimp can I keep in a 40-liter (9 gallons) aquarium?

There should be a maximum of twenty shrimp, provided they are dwarf shrimp. Larger shrimp will need more space, of course.

My water is too hard, but my shrimp need soft water. What can I do?

Water hardness can be softened by using osmosis water and liquid mineral salt. The mineral salt should only affect the water hardness and not the carbonate hardness. The exact mixing ratio can be found in the respective product instructions. There are also hard water salts that can be used if the water is too soft.

Does my aquarium need to be illuminated?

No, actually not. The shrimp do not need any special light, but possibly the plants, if particularly demanding plants have been selected. Previously we have covered simple beginner plants that are very hardy.

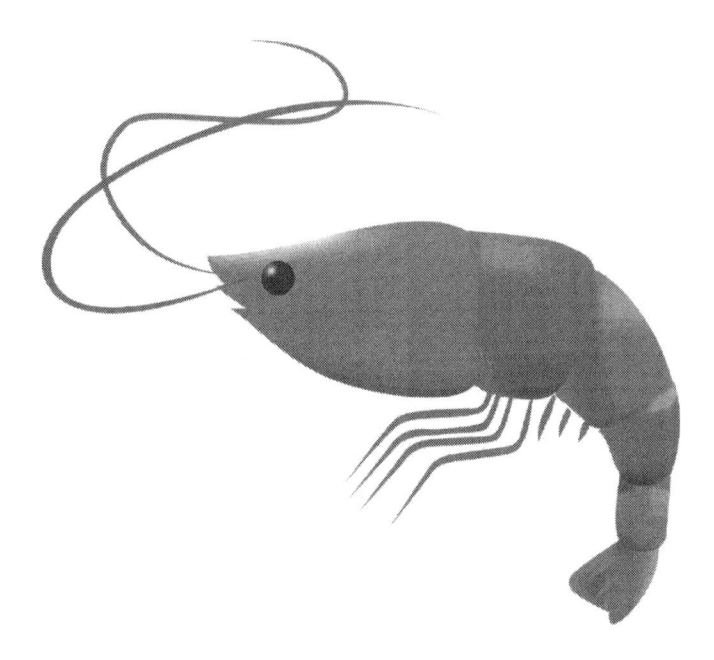

© pcasadofernandez

Does an aquarium for Amano shrimp need to be larger?

Yes, please. Amano shrimp are extremely keen swimmers, so they should be provided with even more space so that they can develop freely and swim around happily. For Amano shrimp, the aquarium should have an edge length of at least 60 centimeters (25 inches). In addition, Amano shrimp grow larger than many other shrimp.

Which substrate is best?

This question cannot be answered unequivocally, as recommendations for this vary from country to country. In general, it can be said that you are well advised to use gravel, which has a fine grain size. Fine sand is also a possible soil substrate. If you decide to use gravel, it should not only be fine, but also natural. Colored gravel looks pretty, but in many cases releases toxins into the water through the coloring.

How expensive are shrimps to buy?

The prices for the shrimp themselves vary extremely depending on the species desired. Common species, whose breeding is very fast and uncomplicated, and which do not have any special characteristics, are already available from fifty cents per animal. However, if you want to buy special shrimps, for example exquisite Caridina shrimps, which have a special pattern, their breeding is more complicated and costly, so that such an exclusive shrimp can even cost around five hundred euros. However, this is neither necessary nor useful for beginners, who are initially well advised with the most common species.

For which shrimp species is the use of osmosis water recommended?

For example, for the Caridina shrimp Taiwan Bee or Red Bee.

My shrimp are quite transparent, but I don't see any blood. Do they not have any?

Shrimp do not have red blood like we do, but instead have hemolymph. This is a fluid that transports oxygen throughout the body. The oxygen transporter in them is hemocyanin.

How old do shrimp live?

This varies depending on the species and, of course, the husbandry conditions. As a rule, shrimp live between one and seven years. Some species, such as the Hawaiian Red, can even live about twenty years.

How long have shrimp been around?

Oh, shrimp have been around for many millions of years! In 2010, researchers recorded an incredible fossil find, as they discovered the fossilization of a shrimp that is already 360 million years old. It was the shrimp species "Aciculopoda mapesi" (named after its discoverer) and the researchers were able to determine that shrimp have hardly changed up to the present day. The fossil was found in Oklahoma in the United States of America, and it is eight centimeters (three inches) in size.

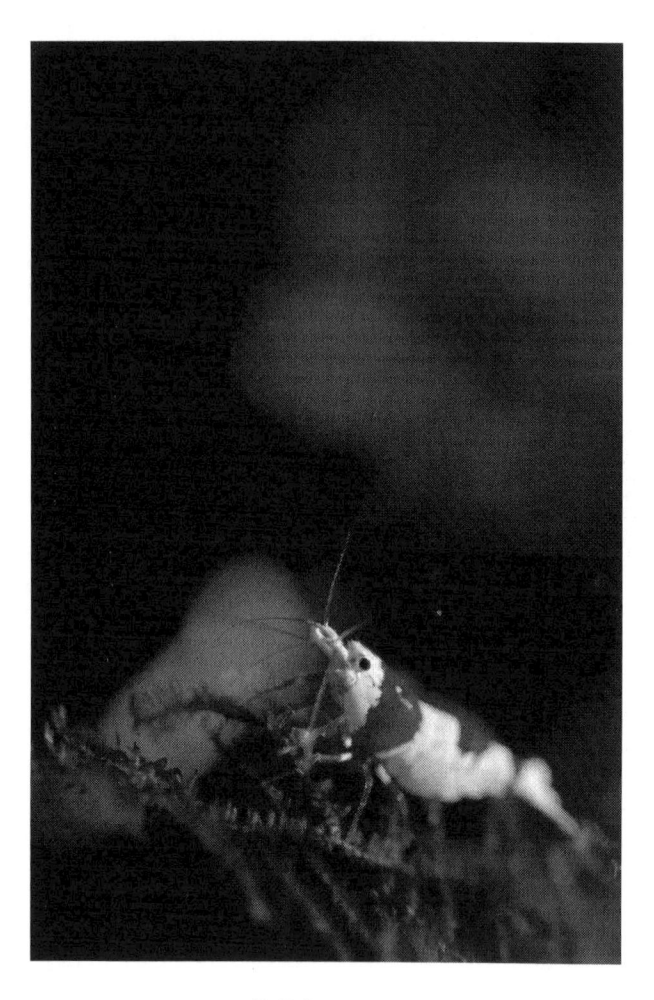

© Ishman000

Dear Readers ♥

For independent authors, product reviews are the foundation of a book's success. That is why we depend on your reviews.

This helps not only the authors, but of course also future readers and especially the animals!

Therefore, I should be grateful for a little review on this book. Thank you so much for your support! 😊

I wish you all the best, much joy with your pets and stay healthy!

(c) Królestwo_Nauki

Legal Notice

This book is protected by copyright. Reproduction by third parties is prohibited. Use or distribution by unauthorised third parties in any printed, audio-visual, audio or other media is prohibited. All rights remain solely with the author.

Author: Alina Daria Djavidrad

Contact: Wahlerstraße 1, 40472 Düsseldorf, Germany

© 2022 Alina Daria Djavidrad

1st edition (2022)

© *Ishman000*

Room for Notes

Printed in Great Britain
by Amazon